Samuel French Acting Edition

Facing Our T
Short Plays on
Race, and Priv

Night Vision
Dominique Morisseau

Some Other Kid
A. Rey Pamatmat

Colored
Winter Miller

The Ballad of George Zimmerman
Dan O'Brien & Quetzal Flores

Dressing
Mona Mansour & Tala Manassah

No More Monsters Here
Marcus Gardley

SAMUELFRENCH.COM   SAMUELFRENCH.CO.UK

FOR PRODUCTION ENQUIRIES

UNITED STATES AND CANADA
Info@SamuelFrench.com
1-866-598-8449

UNITED KINGDOM AND EUROPE
Plays@SamuelFrench.co.uk
020-7255-4302

Each title is subject to availability from Samuel French, depending upon
country of performance. Please be aware that *FACING OUR TRUTH* may
not be licensed by Samuel French in your territory. Professional and
amateur producers should contact the nearest Samuel French office or
licensing partner to verify availability.

MUSIC USE NOTE

Licensees are solely responsible for obtaining formal written permission from copyright owners to use copyrighted music in the performance of this play and are strongly cautioned to do so. If no such permission is obtained by the licensee, then the licensee must use only original music that the licensee owns and controls. Licensees are solely responsible and liable for all music clearances and shall indemnify the copyright owners of the play(s) and their licensing agent, Samuel French, against any costs, expenses, losses and liabilities arising from the use of music by licensees. Please contact the appropriate music licensing authority in your territory for the rights to any incidental music.

IMPORTANT BILLING AND CREDIT REQUIREMENTS

If you have obtained performance rights to this title, please refer to your licensing agreement for important billing and credit requirements.

FACING OUR TRUTH: 10-MINUTE PLAYS ON TRAYVON, RACE AND PRIVILEGE was originally presented at the Martin Segal Theatre Center at CUNY Graduate Center in association with The New Black Fest (Keith Josef Adkins, Artistic Director) in New York City on December 5, 2013.

NIGHT VISION
directed by Kamilah Forbes

AYANNA..Heather Alicia Simms
EZRA.. Curtis McClarin

SOME OTHER KID
directed by Ira Kip

OWEN ....Jamal Mallory-McCree
ANDRE ....Joshua Boone
ELISSA..Shannon Tyo

COLORED
directed by Kamilah Forbes

BLUE.. Nadia Bowers
ALSO BLUE...Jack Koenig
GREEN .... Kim Brockington
PURPLE...Amy Goldberger
YELLOW ....Jamal Mallory-McCree
PINK ....Shannon Tyo
RED ....Joshua Boone

THE BALLAD OF GEORGE ZIMMERMAN
directed by Ira Kip

GEORGE ZIMMERMAN .... Bobby Moreno
TRAYVON ....Joshua Boone
POLICE OFFICER...................................Jack Koenig

DRESSING
directed by Kamilah Forbes

MOM .... Kim Brockington
SON ....Jamal Mallory-McCree

NO MORE MONSTERS HERE
directed by Kamilah Forbes

REBECCA .... Nadia Bowers
DOC .... Curtis McClarin
GREATEST-GRAND/OOKIE ....Heather Alicia Simms

FACING OUR TRUTH was commissioned by The New Black Fest.

TABLE OF CONTENTS

FOREWORD

by Keith Josef Adkins
Artistic Director of The New Black Fest

Facing Our Truth: Ten-Minute Plays
on Trayvon, Race, and Privilege

Trayvon Martin, Michael Brown, Aura Rosser, Rekia Boyd and Eric Garner (among others) were all recently shot and killed by police or disgruntled citizens in the streets of America. Of course they were not the first to lose their lives at the hands of white police or citizens. There was Emmett Till, Mary Turner and Marie Scott – all killed (or lynched) during a time when white authority and sometimes whim took precedence over any forms of justice or logic.

This country has a very complicated relationship with race and privilege. There's no way around it. It has an impact on whose lives we deem suspect and expendable and whose we do not. Some of us can certainly ignore this, but like most repressed conditions, it has a way of resurfacing and demanding full, toxic attention.

As a kid growing up in Cincinnati, Ohio that complicated relationship was always evident. I recall my paternal grandfather, a Baptist pastor, meeting with Civil Rights Activist Reverend Fred Shuttlesworth on several occasions to discuss ongoing racial inequities in town. I recall hanging out with a group of mostly-white friends in San Francisco's neo-bohemian Upper Haight when the police questioned only me about a robbery at a nearby cafe. But it's the story of my grand-uncle that resonates the most. He refused to let a group of white men enter his home as they sought an alleged runaway thief (molasses was his crime). The refusal resulted in the white men returning and hanging my grand-uncle from a tree as just punishment for his disrespect.

These types of testaments play a big part in the general consciousness and culture of black life in this country. They are stories that serve as warnings and strength-builders. They are usually stories and incidents that remain the burden of black people. However, when the Zimmerman verdict was announced I knew I had enough of carrying that burden alone. I wanted to know and hear all Americans take some accountability for how race and privilege continues to impact and shape us.

So, through The New Black Fest, I sought out some peers representing every possible demographic in hopes they would share my concern and passion. Peers who I knew would offer some perspective or observation that would hold all of us accountable for the legacy of privilege and its impact on black expendability. The New Black Fest's *Facing Our Truth: 10-Minute Plays on Trayvon, Race and Privilege* is an attempt to share the burden, to have a collective conversation about how important it is we all look at this toxic legacy and how to take responsibility in stopping the horror it continues to create.

NOTE ON PERFORMANCE

The playwrights involved in FACING OUR TRUTH:
10-MINUTE PLAYS ON TRAYVON, RACE, AND PRIVILEGE
prefer, in all instances possible, that the plays be performed as
a unit.

Night Vision

Dominique Morisseau

CHARACTER DESCRIPTION

AYANNA – Black woman, mid-late 30s. Pregnant. Hyper-sensitive. Over stuffed with book-quotes and clinical terminology. Wife of Ezra.

EZRA – Black man, late 30s. Steady. Calming. Thoughtful. A loving husband with one eye always on the streets around him. Husband of Ayanna.

SETTING

Bed Stuy. Brooklyn. Present. A cool autumn night.

ABOUT THE PLAYWRIGHT

Dominique Morisseau, Playwright/Actress, is alumnus of the Public Theater Emerging Writer's Group, Women's Project Lab, and Lark Playwrights Workshop. Credits include: *Skeleton Crew* (Sundance; Lark Barebones); *Detroit '67* (Public Theater, Classical Theatre of Harlem/ NBT); *Sunset Baby* (Gate Theater; LAByrinth Theatre); *Follow Me To Nellie's* (O'Neill; Premiere Stages). She has produced other original works with the Hip Hop Theater Festival, Penn State University, American Theatre of Harlem, and The New Group. Her three-play cycle, entitled "The Detroit Projects" includes *Detroit '67, Paradise Blue* (developed with Voice and Vision, Hansberry Project, NYTW, McCarter Theatre, Williamstown Theatre Festival, and the Public Theater), and *Skeleton Crew*. Awards: Jane Chambers Playwriting Award, two-time NAACP Image Award, Primus Prize commendation, Stavis Playwriting Award, Spirit of Detroit Award, U of M Emerging Leader Award, Weissberger Award, PoNY Fellowship, Sky-Cooper New American Play Prize, and the Edward M. Kennedy Prize for Drama

(Lights up on the living room of a Brooklyn apartment. Somewhere, importantly: a black hooded sweatshirt. **AYANNA**, *pregnant, enters with her husband* **EZRA**.)*

AYANNA. I cannot fucking believe that.

EZRA. Man was sick.

AYANNA. Man wasn't a man. Man was twisted.

EZRA. Unhealthy.

AYANNA. I'm still shaking.

EZRA. Sit down baby.

AYANNA. I don't want to sit down. I want to find him and kick his ass. I want to –

EZRA. Sit down baby.

AYANNA. Aren't you upset?

EZRA. I'm a lot of things.

AYANNA. I'm hurt. I'm angry. I'm disgusted. I have to pee. I want to find him and kick his ass.

EZRA. You're not going back out there baby.

AYANNA. Then you should go out there.

EZRA. I should go back out there???

AYANNA. Maybe.

EZRA. You want me to go out there and kick his ass?

AYANNA. Maybe.

EZRA. What if he has a gun?

AYANNA. I don't know.

EZRA. Me neither.

   (Beat.)

AYANNA. It was like…was he punching on her?

EZRA. I couldn't really see. Could you?

AYANNA. It looked like he was punching on her.

EZRA. But could you see?

AYANNA. Not completely.

EZRA. Me neither.

   (A moment.)

   I should've kicked his ass. I hesitated.

AYANNA. Why'd you hesitate?

EZRA. I just did.

AYANNA. I'm calling the police.

EZRA. Yeah?

AYANNA. What else can I do?

EZRA. You? Nothing. Me? I can go find him.

AYANNA. No. You're not a fucking vigilante.

EZRA. Didn't you just say – –

AYANNA. I wasn't serious. *You're* serious. I don't want you
   hunting anyone. What if you become the prey?

EZRA. Then call the cops.

AYANNA. I'm calling the cops.

   (**AYANNA** *pulls out her cell.* **EZRA** *peers out of the
   window.*)

EZRA. *(almost to himself)* It's the darkness out there. You
   could get swallowed by it. Goddamn busted streetlight.
   Been half a year and they haven't fixed it.

AYANNA. *(into the phone)* Hi, yes, I want to report a situation
   I just witnessed. A man was beating his girlfriend.
   She was screaming and he – Yes. Yes, I'm sure he was
   beating her. I'm sure. And she was screaming and then
   he took off and ran down the block – Yes. Yes, okay.
   He was a…he was wearing a hooded sweatshirt. It was
   covering his face, but I think it was red. Yes. And his
   pants were dipped low…um…below his waist. He had
   on sneakers. He took off running toward Marcy and
   Green. You could still catch him if you hurry. He was
   a…young… Black –

EZRA. Wait, baby – hold on now. Are you sure???

AYANNA. *(cupping the phone)* What?

EZRA. He was Black?

AYANNA. Yes, I'm sure. My memory is… I'm sure.

EZRA. Are you??? Cuz I'm not.

AYANNA. You're not? *(into the phone)* Yes, I'm still here. Give me a sec. *(cups the phone)* What are you talking about?

EZRA. I thought the sweatshirt was green.

AYANNA. It was red.

EZRA. Are you sure?

AYANNA. Yes! I'm – shit, I'm sure! *(into the phone)* Yes, he ran on foot. We screamed and he ran on foot. My husband yelled. Scared him off. She um, the girl ran too. Into a home. Yes, sure. Okay. Thank you. Uh, no. Anonymous please. Yes. No problem.

(**AYANNA** *hangs up. She looks at* **EZRA**.)

You trying to freak me out?

EZRA. I don't remember red.

AYANNA. Ezra, are you kidding me? The sweatshirt was…

EZRA. …green. Ayanna. It was green.

AYANNA. Fuck, was it?

EZRA. Thats what I remember seeing.

AYANNA. No. That's not right. How could that be right? The streetlight near him wasn't even working. He was in the shadows. I remember red because when he ran, he fell into some headlights for a second. I remember thinking he looked like the devil.

EZRA. The devil?

AYANNA. That's what I was thinking. So it had to be red.

EZRA. I remember green. I remember thinking when he fell into that pool of light that he looked pale underneath all that green.

AYANNA. Pale?

EZRA. That's what I remember thinking.

AYANNA. Could hardly see his face. It was too dark.

EZRA. Then how did you know he was Black?

AYANNA. I…

(A moment.)

AYANNA. What's happening right now?

EZRA. What do you mean?

AYANNA. I called the cops. Was I not supposed to call the cops?

EZRA. No. You can call the cops. You did. You called the cops.

AYANNA. So then what's with the – I mean, why are you doubting me?

EZRA. I'm not doubting you, baby. I'm questioning you. Big difference.

AYANNA. But what in the – what for?

EZRA. Because you aren't sure. For this you have to be. It costs too much to be wrong.

AYANNA. No, I was sure. I was sure. I *felt* sure.

EZRA. But you aren't.

(Beat.)

AYANNA. It's cold in this fucking apartment.

EZRA. I closed the window. Getting chilly out there.

AYANNA. I can't sit still. I'm going to shake myself into oblivion.

EZRA. Sit down. You're upset. You're moving too much. Just sit down.

AYANNA. Hypothyroidism.

EZRA. Don't diagnose yourself right now, baby.

AYANNA. It's a risk. All my books say so. Not good for the baby. *(shift)* I'm all fucking confused now.

EZRA. Stop cussing. Not good for the baby.

AYANNA. I won't stop cussing. Fucking shit fuck. The baby knows when I'm thinking it anyway. He might as well get familiar with the fuckery of the world now.

EZRA. You're not helping anything right now, Ayanna. That's not helping.

AYANNA. I'm not helping? I tried to help. You told me I was wrong.

EZRA. I didn't – I didn't say you were wrong. I just asked if you were sure.

AYANNA. Goddammit Ezra! How am I supposed to be sure??? It's dark.

EZRA. It's nighttime. It's supposed to be dark. Now a brother is a hazard if he walks around at night? Should we carry a label? Caution. Objects appear darker than they really are.

AYANNA. I don't know. Someone was beating a woman. Someone was beating on a woman!!! What am I supposed to do? What if that wasn't his girlfriend? What if he was trying to rape her? What if you hadn't yelled and I hadn't screamed from a distance for him to STOP? What if he beat her to death? Should I not have – should I not try to send the police after him? Should I not have tried to describe him like I remember?

EZRA. Even if your memory is blurred? Even if it's clouded with emotion? Not for one second did I look at that man and think he was Black. Or even young. He was buried in clothing. I didn't know what race he was. He was a blur of half a man. A colorless half a man.

AYANNA. That belongs in jail.

EZRA. That maybe needed some help.

AYANNA. Needed some help?

EZRA. Maybe was homeless and insane or on drugs or high. Maybe was desperate and trying to rob her. Maybe was a kid in trouble – misguided. Maybe –

AYANNA. Maybe was an asshole that needed to be locked away.

EZRA. Maybe.

(*Beat.*)

AYANNA. I'm going to make some tea. Do you want some tea?

EZRA. No.

AYANNA. Are you…are you upset? With me?

EZRA. No. I'm just – no.

AYANNA. I thought he was. He looked like – the way he was dressed. I didn't even consider that he wasn't. Until you got me confused. I didn't even consider for a second.

EZRA. That's the itch right there.

AYANNA. What's the itch?

EZRA. That you didn't even consider – there was no possibility of it being another – in your mind, we're the default. How are we your default?

AYANNA. Ezra, I'm on your team. You know that, right? You and me, husband and wife. The father of my future son. We're going to have a son. I wouldn't – We're going to have a son. I'm on your side. I'm also one of "us." I wouldn't –

EZRA. I know.

AYANNA. Ethno-cultural empathy.

EZRA. What?

AYANNA. In my reading. You're more likely to have empathy for someone who looks like you. Shares your same background. Walked a mile in your shoes. You're concerned about the brother. Concerned that he may be getting a bad rep. I get it. Meanwhile you haven't said one thing about the woman. Even wondered if she was ok.

EZRA. That's what you think of me? That I don't care about her? That I wasn't worried about her getting the life knocked out of her? Why do you think I yelled?

AYANNA. Why didn't you chase him?

EZRA. And what should I have done with you? Leave you? In the middle of Green Ave in the dark? Pregnant and alone? That's the man you want to have a child with?

AYANNA. No.

(Beat.)

EZRA. I need to take a walk.

AYANNA. You're going to leave? While I'm emotional???

EZRA. No baby, not leaving. Just stepping out. Need some air. Come back. Rub your feet. Draw you a bath. Okay?

(EZRA grabs his hooded sweatshirt.)

AYANNA. You're not going to – You're not going to wear that.

EZRA. It's getting chilly out there.

AYANNA. Not tonight. Not tonight.

EZRA. It's all I have. This and a winter coat. I'm supposed to carry that weight now? It's supposed to be my burden to change my attire now?

AYANNA. You're going to make me insane. You're going to make me pee on myself from nervousness. You're going to send me into early labor. You're going to make me cuss – a lot.

EZRA. I'm just going to take a walk, baby. Come back. Put you to bed. Just wanna go make sure everything is okay out there. That's all. You stay here. Rest.

(EZRA heads to the door. Looks at AYANNA.)

Listen…if you're sure, then I trust you. I stand by what you saw.

(He walks over. Kisses her on the forehead, and leaves out.)

(A moment. She peers out of the window.)

(Flash of police car lights. Sirens.)

(Suddenly a kick in her stomach. Intuition. She grabs her belly urgently.)

AYANNA. Oh God… I'm not sure…

(She holds her breath – hands over her heart. And waits on EZRA to return.)

End of Play

Some Other Kid

A. Rey Pamatmat

CAST

(in order of appearance)

ELISSA – 17, any race (non-white), some kid
ANDRE – 17, African-American, some other kid
OWEN – 17, any race, their friend

TIME

Some day at the end of some summer.

PLACE

Some American suburb.

ABOUT THE PLAYWRIGHT

A. Rey Pamatmat's play *after all the terrible things I do* premiered at the Milwaukee Repertory Theatre and was subsequently produced at The Huntington Theatre in May 2015. His play *A Power Play; Or, What's-its-name* was presented at the 2014 O'Neill Playwrights Conference, his second residency there after *Thunder Above, Deeps Below* in 2008. Rey's play *Edith Can Shoot Things and Hit Them* premiered at the Humana Festival, received the Steinberg/ATCA New Play Citation and nominations for 2013 GLAAD Media and Lambda Literary Awards, and was featured at Guadalajara's 2014 Semana Internacional de la Dramaturgia. Productions: *Thunder Above, Deeps Below* (Second Generation), *A Spare Me* (Waterwell), *DEVIANT* (the Vortex), *High/Limbo/High* (HERE); awards: '12–'13 Hodder Fellowship, '11–'12 PoNY Fellowship, Princess Grace Award, Princess Grace Special Projects Grant, NYFA Playwriting Fellowship, E.S.T./Sloan Grant. Rey is Co-Director of the Ma-Yi Writer's Lab. BFA: NYU, MFA: Yale School of Drama.

(**ELISSA,** *alone.*)

ELISSA. *(to the audience)* I make these on my computer at home.

(**ELISSA** *produces three large, round, glossy stickers. The art on them looks like something between a corporate logo and graffiti. They're well designed.*)

(to the audience) People are always trying to sell you shit. Not me. I'm trying to remind you about something you already have.

I go out and stick these places. Sometimes I stick them on things that are cool, you know, that I like. Like Facebook or something, but in the real world. Like there's this community garden at the Episcopal Church, and I put a dollar in the donation box that had this stuck on it.

(She holds up a Dream sticker.)

(to the audience) "Dream." This one means dream.

Sometimes I want to say, "This ain't right." Like if there's a violent movie poster, I stick this one on it to remind people that they can have love, too.

(A Love sticker.)

(to the audience) "Love."

Or if a company says they're selling you freedom, but really they're selling you a shoe, then I stick this one on it to remind you of what you already have.

(A Power sticker.)

(to the audience) "Power."

I made .JPEGs, too.

Sometimes, when something awful has happened like an amazing woman is assassinated or a revolution goes wrong or a neighbor doesn't act neighborly, I tweet a link to a page filled with these pictures. A Power, Dream, or Love bomb to remind everyone that these things are already inside them, waiting to be exercised. Or at least remembered.

Because I don't want to sell you shit. You have everything you need in what you already are.

(Lights shift to another part of the stage where **ANDRE** *and* **OWEN** *play video games together in* **ANDRE***'s dad's living room.)*

ANDRE. She's like my sister, Owen. And you grew up with her, too.

OWEN. Not like you did. We weren't close like that.

ANDRE. You want to ask out your sister?

OWEN. No, I want to ask out Elissa who I grew up with but am not related to. Not my sister. More like a cousin.

ANDRE. First or second?

OWEN. Shut up.

ANDRE. First cousin is still illegal.

OWEN. BUT SHE'S NOT REALLY MY COUSIN OR MY SISTER. Look: I don't want to ruin shit.

ANDRE. I don't control Elissa.

OWEN. But do you think it would make things weird? Would you be cool?

ANDRE. If you think you have a chance, you don't need my permission.

OWEN. You just said she's like your sister.

ANDRE. But she's not.

OWEN. Jesus fucking – FUCK YOU.

*(***ANDRE*** starts cracking up.)*

ANDRE. Look, Elissa can take care of herself. Do what you want to do.

OWEN. Our last year has to be epic. Before you leave for your fancy school. I don't want to mess it up.

ANDRE. It's not fancy. And it's only five hours away. I'm not going to New Zealand or something.

(**ELISSA** *moves into their space.*)

ELISSA. Who's going to New Zealand?

OWEN. Andre is, when he goes to his fancy school.

ELISSA. I know you didn't do well in geography, but you might want to look at a map.

OWEN. I don't need a map to know I'm not going where Andre's going.

ELISSA. Right? Early admission. Honor student. You may even end up valedictorian, Andre.

ANDRE. Where have you been? Sticking stickers to save the world?

ELISSA. Something like that. I'll save the world, and you'll change it into something worth saving.

ANDRE. I'm not changing shit. I just want everyone to have a little fun.

OWEN. *(out of nowhere)* I might become a vegetarian. You know, like stop eating meat.

ELISSA. What? Why?

ANDRE. You can't be a vegetarian after everything you've done.

OWEN. What does that mean?

ANDRE. Fish baseball.

ELISSA. "Fish baseball?"

(*Lights shift as* **OWEN** *leaves the scene and speaks to the audience.*)

OWEN. *(to the audience)* My cousin Geo is a real prick.

There was this cat once that was, you know, just around. Stray, indoor/outdoor, what have you. I don't think he belonged to anyone, or maybe I just made it like that in my head because of what happened.

Which is this.

My prick cousin stalked this cat, like hunted it, and poked it with sticks and shit. Real mature, right? "Here, kitty, kitty, look at this stick." And then: poke or whack or smack. And I'd be all, "Leave the cat alone. He didn't do shit." And Geo would say, "She don't belong here. This isn't her territory."

The cat's not stupid, though. My cousin keeps going and going and going after it. Then one day, the cat gets poked, he jumps in the air, runs up the stick like kung fu shit, and slashes Geo across the face.

He's bleeding. There's skin hanging off. So my prick cousin hunts the cat down and clubs the shit out of him.

Kills him.

And when people are like, "Dude, you killed a cat?" Geo goes, "Look what it did to my face! Self defense."

And all I think is, "Yeah. The cat can say self defense for slashing your face, but all you can say is you're a stupid prick for hunting a cat who didn't do shit to anyone."

(OWEN rejoins the scene.)

ANDRE. Your past will always catch up to you.

OWEN. Especially if your so-called friends keep dragging you back.

ELISSA. Don't make me Google this shit.

ANDRE. You won't find it. Our stupidity is beyond even the Internet.

OWEN. Andre, Elissa doesn't need / to hear –

ELISSA. Tell me, or I'm going home.

OWEN. Fish baseball is / when you go –

ANDRE. You are too easy.

OWEN. Your mom is.

ANDRE. You sure this is your chance? Fish baseball?

ELISSA. Chance?

(Five seconds.)

ANDRE. Never mind.

ELISSA. Uh-huh.

OWEN. Fish baseball is when you go fishing, and you catch one that's too small. But instead of throwing it back, you get your friend to pitch it to you, and you hit it with a bat.

ANDRE. And your friend ends up with fish guts all over him.

(*Five seconds.*)

ELISSA. You are both retarded.

(**ANDRE** *and* **OWEN** *crack up.*)

They're small, because they're babies. You killed babies.

OWEN. They die anyway.

ELISSA. Everything dies anyway. Is that going to be your excuse when you go on a shooting spree?

OWEN. No, but even if you throw them back. By the time you get the hook out, most times they're already dead.

ELISSA. So you torture them instead?

ANDRE. No, they're doomed. We just put them out of their misery.

OWEN. With a bat.

(**ANDRE** *mimes a pitch;* **OWEN** *hits. They crack up again.*

ELISSA. Bye.

OWEN. No, no, no, no, no. We were – I was laughing at what a stupid kid I was. Not at killing babies.

ANDRE. I remember plenty of stupid kid things you did before you decided to save the world.

ELISSA. DO. NOT.

OWEN. This is my point, right? I am more conscious now of…of shit. I would never play fish baseball now. So… vegetarianism.

ANDRE. You're just tired of throwing out shirts covered in fish guts.

OWEN. Even if I was a stupid kid, now I'm not. I won't grow up to become some prick; I can do shit for the world, too.

*(Lights shift as **ANDRE** leaves the scene and speaks to the audience.)*

ANDRE. *(to the audience)* Everything is stupid. That's what people don't get. No one is a better person. Elissa is good at drawing. Owen is good at swimming and track and baseball. And I'm good at school.

School isn't about knowing the shit they're telling you. It's about playing the game. I'm not a super genius; there's no big secret; I'm just some kid. The game I happen to like playing is school. It's all about what's fun.

And they sell us this bullshit about how special we are, and so we try to be special. But seriously: ninety percent of the world is fuck ups. I don't have a citation for that from the American Journal of Fucked Upedness, but we all know it's true. And yet the world still turns.

I'm not special. The world right now happens to value the game I'm good at playing. Later on, maybe I won't mean shit – nothing I do or have done, maybe none of it will mean shit.

And that's cool, because I already know it, and it's a messed up idea anyway. Believing one person is more special than another leads you down a road where other people aren't special. Are disposable. And no one is disposable.

Those ideas are connected, so we've got to give them both up. One day I'm special. The next day it'll be some other kid. One day some other kid is disposable. The next day…

That's fucked up. We're all just trying to live our lives. Our regular lives. No one's life is better or more important than anyone else's.

*(**ANDRE** rejoins the scene.)*

When did I ever say you couldn't do shit for the world?

OWEN. You and Elissa are –

ELISSA. Are just the same as you. Why is this even a discussion? Obviously, we are all amazing.

(**ELISSA** *sticks a Power sticker on* **OWEN**'s *forehead.*)

See?

ANDRE. I'm going to the 7-11. Anyone need anything?

OWEN. Just give me my chance. You know what I need.

ANDRE. Well, I'm not a social worker, so you better tell an adult you trust if your mommy's boyfriends are still looking at you in a way that makes you uncomfortable.

OWEN. Why does everything have to become an insult to my mom?

ANDRE. That was an insult to your mom's boyfriends.

OWEN. Iced tea. Bitch.

ANDRE. Don't call me bitch. I'm not your mom.

OWEN. Stop it. You know what I need.

(**OWEN**'s *eyes point to* **ELISSA**.)

ANDRE. Need anything, Elissa?

ELISSA. Sour Patch Kids. I drove here from school, so my car is in your driveway.

ANDRE. I want to walk.

ELISSA. It's night.

ANDRE. *(hinting to* **OWEN***)* It's ten minutes there and back. I'm walking.

(back to **ELISSA***)*

And there's a crazy gate around the entire neighborhood to keep our houses safe as houses.

(**ANDRE** *pulls a hoodie on.*)

Iced tea and Sour Patch Kids. Anything else? Last chance.

(to **OWEN***)*

If there's something you want, this is your chance.

(**OWEN** *smiles.*)

All right. Ten minutes.

(**ANDRE** *goes.*)

ELISSA. What are you going to do without him?

OWEN. Same as you, I guess.

ELISSA. You don't need him to hold your hand.

OWEN. Then who's going to do it?

ELISSA. I just mean: I'm not stupid.

OWEN. I get it. I mean, yeah. I know.

ELISSA. So then, what are you two talking about?

OWEN. You.

ELISSA. Me?

OWEN. And me.

ELISSA. Me and you?

OWEN. Yeah.

ELISSA. Oh. Me and you.

OWEN. Maybe.

ELISSA. What brought this on?

OWEN. I don't know. You just…you always know how to make me feel good. I noticed that you always make me feel good.

(**OWEN** *takes the Power sticker off his forehead, and sticks it on his shirt, over his heart.* **ELISSA** *smiles.*)

ELISSA. Are you sure "Power" is the one you got for that? Maybe all you got is "Dream."

OWEN. Maybe it's the other one. What's the third one? Oh, yeah…

(**OWEN** *leans in to kiss her, just as he does…*)

(*The sound of a gunshot.*)

(*Sirens and flashing lights as lights shift to another part of the stage where* **ANDRE** *lays, shot to death.*)

(**ELISSA** *and* **OWEN** *go to him.* **OWEN** *starts to sob.*)

(**ELISSA** *sticks a Love sticker on* **ANDRE**'s *corpse. She sticks a Dream sticker on her own forehead.*)

(ELISSA takes OWEN's hand and they walk toward the audience. She takes out a Power sticker and holds it out to the audience. OWEN takes the Power sticker off his shirt and holds it out to the audience as well. Perhaps the equivalent of ELISSA's Internet "Power Bomb" is set – the stage fills with the Power symbol projected over and over again or Power stickers fall from above onto the audience.)

End of Play

End of Play

Colored

Winter Miller

ACKNOWLEDGMENTS

Thank you to Keith Josef Adkins and The New Black Fest for clear and steady vision. Appreciation and affection to this entire crew of writers. Thank you to four writers who encouraged me to go all in: Alice Tuan, Aditi Kapil, Shontina Vernon and Carson Kreitzer. And for all of you whom I've met (and those I haven't) who walk the line: you are my teachers. Gratitude for the artists upon whose shoulders I stand: Baraka, Cleage, Kennedy, Nottage, Shange, Lorde, Rich, Morrison, Wallace, Hansberry and so many more, including Russell G. Jones and the Blindspot.

CHARACTERS

BLUE – Woman

ALSO BLUE – Man

GREEN – Woman

PURPLE – Woman

YELLOW – Boy, 15

PINK – Boy, 16

RED – Boy, 15

INDIGO – Woman

[This role is optional, depending if you have resources.]++

TEAL – Woman

[This role is optional, depending if you have resources.]++

*The above colors of the characters must be made known to the audience by some method; please use your imagination.

++ Indigo and Teal represent the bystander, and as such are important, but if you don't have the cast, you can do just one or none.

TIME AND PLACE

Day, an outdoor subway platform in Brooklyn.

NOTES

If your school or community has restrictions on curse words, I'd rather you present the play than not, so please be creative about what words you choose to substitute while maintaining the TENSION between the different characters and the rising UGLINESS. Better yet, use the language as written and have a conversation among your group and your audience about the impulse to step back from some words and not others.

If you want to be adventurous and you have the luxury of time or you're doing this play as an exercise, try running it through at least twice, with characters of different races switching roles.

A "/" means the second person begins speaking before the first person has stopped. This contributes to the SPEED.

The pacing must move FAST like a train. Only if there is a stated pause or rest should there be space between dialogue.

The Satie composition is a particular choice but it doesn't have to be this exact one. I picked *Unpleasant Glimpses #3, Fugue for Piano* because Satie's irreverence interested me and in particular, the fugue felt right tonally and narratively. A director may play around with the music choice but stay in the classical piano sound, please. Here's a little more background on why I chose a fugue.

1. A fugue usually has three sections: an exposition, a development, and a recapitulation.
2. A period of amnesia during which the affected person seems to be conscious and to make rational decisions: upon recovery, the period is not remembered.

The following text is projected or spoken before the lights come up or actors enter. If the text is spoken, this actor should speak the text as if he IS Pablo Picasso and he means it.

What do you think an artist is? An imbecile who has only eyes if he is a painter, or ears if he is a musician, or a lyre in every chamber of his heart if he is a poet, or even, if he is a boxer, just his muscles?

Far, far from it: at the same time, he is also a political being, constantly aware of the heartbreaking, passionate, or delightful things that happen in the world, shaping himself completely in their image.

How could it be possible to feel no interest in other people, and with a cool indifference to detach yourself from the very life which they bring to you so abundantly?

No, painting is not done to decorate apartments. It is an instrument of war. *– Pablo Picasso.*

ABOUT THE PLAYWRIGHT

Winter Miller is an award-winning playwright and founding member of the Obie-recognized collective 13 Playwrights. She is perhaps best known for her drama *In Darfur* which premiered at The Public Theater, followed by a standing room only performance at their 1800-seat Delacorte Theater in Central Park, a first for a play by a woman. *In Darfur* won the "Two-Headed Challenge" commission from the Guthrie and the Playwrights Center and has been produced nationally. She traveled with her former boss, *New York Times* columnist Nicholas Kristof to the Sudan border to research on the ground. Ms. Miller's full-length plays include: *The Penetration Play, Seed, No One is Forgotten,* and the musical *Amandine.*

The Group Voices of Uganda brought Ms. Miller to northern Uganda to write short plays for a group of youth living in a refugee camp whose lives had been ravaged by the LRA and AIDS. The work is chronicled in the documentary *After Kony: Staging Hope.*

Ms. Miller's monologue *Mother to Son,* is published in Eve Ensler's anthology *A Memory, A Monologue, A Rant and A Prayer* and in the anthology *Best Women's Monologues of The Millennium.* Her prose is published in the anthology *Click: When We Knew We Were Feminists.* She has written for *The New York Times, New York Magazine, The Boston Globe,* among others.

(Lights up:)

(BLUE yells at ALSO BLUE, edges him towards the subway platform exit.)

BLUE. Put your penis away!
Don't you do that / around me!

ALSO BLUE. You don't KNOW what you're / talking about!
(mumbles) Anyhow. What is it because.

BLUE. Nobody wants to see your penis!

ALSO BLUE. You're crazy! /
(mumbles) People who think they know. They don't know. Et cetera.

BLUE. Put your damn penis away!
You're a blue man!
/ Move on out!

ALSO BLUE. Don't get CLOSE UP on me. Come correct.
(mumbles) So, et cetera.

BLUE. / Get off this platform!

ALSO BLUE. *(mumbles) I can be wherever I want. /*
AMERICA is for FREEdom.

BLUE. I'll call the police / on you!

ALSO BLUE. *(half mumbles) Don't know /* WHAT her problem is.

BLUE. With your penis out!
You're a blue man!

(The train arrives.)

(BLUE boards.)

(ALSO BLUE remains on the platform.)

(BLUE turns to yell back at ALSO BLUE.)

BLUE. Taking your penis out – !

    You better put it away!

    Keep it away!

    *(**GREEN** and **PURPLE** board behind **BLUE**.)*

    (The doors close.)

    *(**BLUE** stands still for a moment.)*

    (Pause.)

    *(**BLUE** looks for a seat and takes the nearest one.)*

    *(Pause. **GREEN** sits near her.)*

GREEN. Are you alright?

BLUE. I'm fine.

GREEN. Thank you for saying that…

    – I stood near you… to have your back…

    Speaking up.

    – It's hard.

BLUE. I'm fine.

    He's the one not alright.

    Taking his penis / out.

PURPLE. He's not okay.

    Not right.

    So you tell him.

    *(**PURPLE** sits with **BLUE** and **GREEN**.)*

GREEN. Thank you.

    For all of us.

    You're a strong woman.

    Stuff is…hard.

PURPLE. Would you like some snacks?

    (offers) Here, have some.

BLUE. No thank you.

PURPLE. *(to **GREEN**)* Have some snacks.

    Cashews, raisins, here you have some.

    Try it.

GREEN. Oh, no thank you. That's very kind.

PURPLE. Come I insist.

This is dry mango. Very sweet.

GREEN. Ok, uh, thank you.

(**GREEN** *awkwardly puts her fingers into* **PURPLE***'s snack bag.*)

PURPLE. *(to* **BLUE***)* Here.

You have some mango.

BLUE. Thank you.

(**BLUE** *removes a tissue from her handbag and politely removes a slice of mango.*)

GREEN. I'm sorry, I didn't think to use a tissue!

/ Or pour it?

PURPLE. Not a big deal.

Your hands are clean.

I can tell.

(Rest.)

(The sound of the subway arriving:)

VOICE. *(muffled)* This is *(static)* station. Next stop is *(Static)...*

(Three teenage boys, **YELLOW**, **PINK** *and* **RED** *board. They stand at the other end of the car, immersed in each other, strategizing, joshing.)*

(Two others enter, **INDIGO** *and* **TEAL** *strangers to each other. They sit by themselves with headphones, they will not speak or make eye contact with anyone. They will remain self-absorbed.)*

GREEN. *(to* **BLUE***)* I – uh –

I heard you say to him,

"You're a blue man..."

BLUE. He is a blue man.

GREEN. I was wondering if...his race means something to you?

BLUE. Of course it does. Race is race.

He wants to play the fool –

wave his penis around,

people look and say, "That's what I expect from a blue
man."

…Or some kid sees him and thinks,

"That's what men do."

It troubles us all when one of us does something wrong.

GREEN. That's what I guessed…

I wasn't sure.

For me, if a green man does that,

he doesn't represent ALL green men.

To me:

He's one bad apple.

But it seems a blue man…stands for all blue men.

PURPLE. Yes, what you are saying I think is true with blue
men.

BLUE. My mother told me:

You can be the exception,

or you can be the rule.

PURPLE. I do my work. I go here,

Then I go there.

Bup-bup-bup, bahp. Home.

(Micro beat.)

You don't know when he has a gun or a knife.

Or someone who is just crazy with his fists.

I observe people.

GREEN. I'm not scared of blue men –

I'm scared of poor blue men.

BLUE. –

GREEN. I am scared of poor men.

I am scared of all men.

PURPLE. But you ride the subway.

Am I right?

GREEN. I am not afraid of gay men.

BLUE. Why not?

GREEN. They don't want anything from me.

Like I am invisible.

Or something shiny…to admire?

PURPLE. Oh.

I understand how you mean.

BLUE. Do you have a husband?

GREEN. Me? No.

I did.

He passed.

BLUE. I am sorry.

PURPLE. Me too.

My husband has also passed away.

(Pause.)

I understand.

You have a husband?

BLUE. We aren't together.

Haven't been for years.

*(**PURPLE** nods.)*

(Pause.)

GREEN. …

BLUE. …

PURPLE. …

GREEN. I was glad to see you do it

I can't just ride, I –

I'm always on high alert.

I don't even mean to.

*(**PINK, YELLOW,** and **RED** explode from their tight knot onto the scene.*

PINK. Wassup, wassup, wassup? It's showtime!

YELLOW. What time is it?

RED. Showtime!

PINK. Ladies and… *(notices)* other ladies /

Welcome to the show!

RED. This is the female car.

And us!

But we will not be using profanity.

PINK. We won't offend you.

With this small audience,

y'all realize you will have to represent for the ones who couldn't be here today, the ones who stayed in bed today.

RED. That played hooky today!

They know who they are.

YELLOW. It's shoooooooowtiiiiime!

PINK. Prepare to be inspired to acts of generosity!

RED. (*stadium echo*) Generosity...rosity...rosity...

PURPLE. They have a lot of confidence with this.

(BLUE *shakes her head.*)

GREEN. I like it. But.

I always wonder if they will

hit someone in the head?

YELLOW. (*softly for the other two*) Let's do this...

(*The boys blast Erik Satie's "Unpleasant Glimpses #3, Fugue for Piano" or something of similar intentions.* The first boy's movements are acrobatic, balletic, smooth. The second boy goes and his movements are the opposite, jerky, slow, grounded. The third glides from one end of the car to the other.*)

(*They slip congratulatory high fives to each other.*)

(INDIGO *and* TEAL *remain unchanged.*)

PURPLE. (*claps*) I was entertained. (*She hands over a dollar.*)

PINK. Thank you Miss!

Would you like to donate for the invisible man in the seat next to you?

He couldn't be here today because he got fired from his job –

RED. Then his wife and kids left him because he had no money.

YELLOW. Another American dream: Lost!

PURPLE. One dollar. I am not a rich woman.

GREEN. I have some change. Here.

RED. Miss, I see some green in there,
      don't hold out on / us!

GREEN. Those are fives and tens.
      I need them.

PURPLE. You can have snacks, *(offers)*
      this is mango.

RED. That mango stuff is mad good. *(He reaches his hand to grab.)*

PINK. You need manners, son!
      You can't stick your hand in this nice / lady's food.

PURPLE. I can pour / it.

RED. I'm good, I was / just joking,

PINK. Put your hand out, let her pour / it in.

RED. I don't want any.

GREEN. Don't feel bad. I did that / too.

PINK. Hello, Miss, please contribute to our future college fund?

BLUE. I donate money to excellent charities which help the under-served. I don't give on the subway. But your act was not bad.

PINK. We are the under-served We need to GET served for a change –

RED. Get over-served!

YELLOW. She complimented our act / that's enough.

PINK. We're not selling drugs, we're not hitting you over the head and / robbing you –

YELLOW. Don't run your / mouth man.

RED. We did honest entertainment!

BLUE. I didn't ask for your entertainment.
      I would have been happy to enjoy the quiet.

YELLOW. She's got a point, we were / disturbing the quiet.
      I'm sorry…

RED. She should go to the library for quiet/

PINK. This is a subway!

JGGGGHHHH JGGGGGGGGGGH JGGGGGGGHH /
JGGGGGGHHHH *(imitating the sound of the subway cars)*

RED. It's noisy. Subways are machines.

PINK. We could just take your bag right now.

It's three of you, three of us,

There's no doubt about who would have the problem.

YELLOW. Relax – c'mon –

RED. Why you all up on us? Where's your / loyalty?

YELLOW. I just – we don't need to –

I don't know. /

You know?

PINK. Miss, maybe you're not familiar with the opportunities
for young people like us?

RED. Prison. Murder. Basketball. Football. Baseball. Janitor.

YELLOW. Come on. / You guys, let's –

PINK. The options are –

RED. Half of all homicides are US. But WE don't make up
half the people living in this country. How can you
explain that? / We get targeted.

YELLOW. We got the next car…/ keep it movin'…

PINK. Everybody wants to kill us,

not just the FBI and the CIA.

BLUE. I don't disagree with you there.

PINK. It's insane! She agrees!

So why you have to grip your money so tight,

NOT give to us even though we WORK for / it?

YELLOW. You / can't force somebody.

RED. You work hard for your money and we work hard –

GREEN. Listen.

She has a right not to give.

RED. *(to GREEN)* He's not talking to you. /

I'm not either.

YELLOW. Y'all twistin'.

Nobody gonna give us money if you harassin' / 'em.

PINK. She's got some bullshit attitude / about –

GREEN. You came on this train –

RED. This isn't worth my time.

YELLOW. So let's go.

GREEN. Move along.

BLUE. Let me ask you something.

  Do you think sixty seconds of dancing and jumping is
  worth a dollar?

PINK. / More!

RED. Yes!

BLUE. I make nineteen dollars and twenty cents an hour –

PINK. What's that come out to, / a week?

YELLOW. Next car.

PINK. Wait, she's talking.

BLUE. Every sixty minutes of my seven point five hour day,
  three days a week because they cut back my hours
  from forty to twenty.

YELLOW. We're sorry.

  / He didn't mean to offend you –

RED. No offense –

PINK. I haven't offended anybody.

GREEN. You guys should apologize and move on.

RED. I got no reason to apologize.

PURPLE. Well… You are being disrespectful to her.

  But maybe it's okay if you just go now.

PINK. What did we do that's – / so –

YELLOW. Shut up.

RED. *(to* **YELLOW***)* Chill for a sec. /

  I think there's…

GREEN. Go to the next car.

RED. I don't take orders from you.

PURPLE. Okay, okay… –

BLUE. I wasn't finished.

  My sixty seconds at my job is worth thirty-two cents
  before taxes.

  I am three times your age,

I finished high school and
I have a bachelors degree.

RED. So…?

PINK. You picked the wrong job then.

GREEN. *(mumbled)* Jesus Christ…

BLUE. How long have you been doing your dance moves?
You take classes?
Study at a conservatory?
Put your time in and learn and practice a skill?

RED. It sounds like she's saying we should give her the cup…?

GREEN. You should.

BLUE. I don't want it.

PINK. Here you go.

(He offers her the cup.)

(She doesn't take it.)

(He shakes it.)

(She doesn't move.)

(YELLOW *walks away from them.)*

(PINK *shakes the cup again.)*

BLUE. I earn my own.
No thank you.

GREEN. This isn't cool.
Get out of here.
(about **YELLOW***)* He gets it.

PURPLE. So go somewhere else for your money.

PINK. Yes.
But she has a point.
I bet if we do this for two hours, we make a hundred bucks.
So now I feel bad.

RED. Don't feel bad.
We're working for it.
Don't lose sight, son.

YELLOW. *(mumbles)* I'm going.

GREEN. You don't even pay taxes.

And why aren't you in school today?

RED. Vacation.

GREEN. Spring break was in February, I'm a teacher.

RED. I'm a student.

YELLOW. Let's go / guys…

RED. Our school is off now.

GREEN. Is that so?

What school is that?

PINK. Dalton.

RED. Stupid.

GREEN. You don't need my coins.

(Pause.)

PURPLE. What is Dalton?

GREEN. Fancy private school.

*(**BLUE** shakes her head.)*

BLUE. You see?

RED. See what?

PURPLE. You have my dollar and so does your conscience.

GREEN. You should / be ashamed.

PINK. We all have scholarships! We can't afford / it.

BLUE. / I give to charity because I know it's going to people who need it. / You just confirmed that.

YELLOW. *(points to **RED**)* He's on full scholarship, and we get some financial aid.

PINK. Same diff, he just gets more than we do.

RED. *(justifying to **GREEN**, **PURPLE**, **BLUE**)* I don't have a dad.

BLUE. Pull your pants up. Go to the library or the museum.

*(**PINK** sighs loudly.)*

BLUE. You talk trash, people will treat you like trash.

You have an opportunity most young men like you do not have.

PINK. I got you.

I got you…

PURPLE. Good.

Everybody finally understands each other.

PINK. Yes, this is the "be a credit to your people" speech.

BLUE. *(grabs his hand, misses, holds his arm).* / We need you!

RED. Let go his arm. You don't touch / him –

GREEN. She didn't mean / to –

RED. That's aggressive behavior –

PURPLE. She did not hurt him.

RED. She could have.

YELLOW. This isn't right –

PINK. Let's go.

I hope you're happy with your thirty-two cents a minute part-time-ass-job, soon-to-be-on-unemployment and then food stamps!

What kind of role model are you / gonna be huh?

RED. Bitch will be a welfare queen!

(BLUE goes silent. Sits. Turns away.)

(GREEN stands.)

What are you lookin' at, bitch?

GREEN. Don't call me anything. Don't call her anything –

PINK. *(robot/establishment)* "We will tell you what to say."

"We have the power."

PURPLE. Settle down.

Nobody means anybody any harm.

(YELLOW has moved towards the far door.)

RED. Nobody's doing harm.

She's making assumptions!

Half the murder victims in this country are my people!
I'm sick of being called violent when I just open my mouth to say I object
/ to the way you see me!

PINK. I'm sick of women like you wanna tell us how to be!
Get off my back! / I'm not doing anything wrong!

GREEN. You're being disrespectful!

RED. Who asked you to put your mouth in?

GREEN. I'm not gonna watch while you talk to her like that.

PINK. Obviously, you need this more than us.

(PINK *dumps the cup of money on* BLUE*'s lap.*)

GREEN. You need to get some respect!

PURPLE. I cannot watch.

(*she gets up*) I am sick inside.

(BLUE *stands, the coins jangle and the bills fall to the floor.*)

GREEN. Are you okay?

BLUE. I'm fine. This is my stop.

(*The doors open.* BLUE *exits.*)

PINK. I hope you enjoy the ghetto!

RED. With your government cheese!

(*The train doors remain open.*)

(YELLOW *exits after* BLUE.)

(*He turns and sticks his head back in.*)

YELLOW. She could have been my grandmother.
Or she could have been yours.

(YELLOW *exits. The train doors remain open.*)

VOICE. The train will be moving shortly.
We are being held by the dispatcher.
Thank you for your patience.

PINK. Let's go.

(*He starts to walk off the train.*)

RED. How long you wanna do this?

PINK. Fifty bucks?

GREEN. You should be ashamed.
Your friend at least figured it out.

(They linger in the doorway.)

RED. When I want your opinion, I'll dial a ho.

PURPLE. *(to* **GREEN***)* Not now. Shhh. Nothing.

PINK. That bitch better keep her mouth to herself or she's
not gonna be happy.

PURPLE. Please, go, nobody wants trouble.

GREEN. You're going to get what you deserve.

I work hard not to see kids like you have fucked up
lives, but you ruin it!

For everyone!

You have to poison the well!

And you don't even know it!

PINK. Am I supposed to kiss your ass?

RED. Put your dick up her non-profit ass.

PURPLE. *(to* **GREEN***)* You can take a different train?

I will come with you.

PINK. Oh sit the fuck down.

We aren't going to mess with you.

Some cop would probably kill us.

(They swing out the door and into the next car.)

(offstage:)

What time is it?

RED. It's showtime!

PINK. What time is it?

RED. Shoooooowtiiiiiiime!

(The train doors close.)

*(**GREEN** and **PURPLE** are standing.)*

*(**INDIGO** and **TEAL** are the same as they were at the start
of the scene.)*

End of Play

The Ballad Of George Zimmerman

Text by Dan O'Brien, Music by Quetzal Flores

CHARACTERS

ZIMMERMAN – Late 20s, would call himself Hispanic.

TRAYVON – Late teens, would call himself Black.

OFFICER – Would call herself White.

TIME & PLACE

Most of this takes place in the rain in a backyard at the Retreat at Twin Lakes in Sanford, Florida, February 26, 2012, a little after 7 p.m. – in the ten minutes or so from George Zimmerman's 911 call until Trayvon Martin's death.

The Officer's song at the end reveals that we've been in George Zimmerman's head all along. For the literal-minded, perhaps Zimmerman is getting his gun back at the courthouse.

Only the actor portraying George Zimmerman needs to be able to play the guitar. The others are welcome to augment their performances with percussive elements, such as hand-clapping, feet-stomping, etc.

If no suitable guitar-playing actor can be found, as a last resort an instrumental recording can be provided.

ABOUT THE PLAYWRIGHTS

Dan O'Brien is a playwright, poet, and librettist. His play *The Body of an American* received the inaugural Edward M. Kennedy Prize, the Horton Foote Prize for Outstanding New American Play, the PEN Center USA Award for Drama, the L. Arnold Weissberger Award, and was shortlisted for an Evening Standard Drama Award in the UK. *The Body of an American* premiered at Portland Center Stage, directed by Bill Rauch, and received its European premiere in an extended run at the Gate Theatre in London and *Royal & Derngate* in Northampton, England, directed by James Dacre, and will premiere off-Broadway at Primary Stages in 2016. Previous plays by O'Brien have premiered at Second Stage Theatre, Actors Theatre of Louisville, Williamstown Theatre Festival, Ensemble Studio Theatre, Geva Theatre Center, and elsewhere. O'Brien's debut poetry collection, *War Reporter* (Hanging Loose Press, 2013; CB Editions, 2013), received the UK's prestigious Fenton-Aldeburgh First Collection Prize, and was shortlisted for the Forward Prize for Best First Collection. A new poetry collection entitled *Scarsdale* was published in 2014 by CB Editions in the UK, and in 2015 by Measure Press in the US. O'Brien's libretto for Jonathan Berger's *Visitations* was commissioned by the National Endowment for the Arts and the Andrew W. Mellon Foundation. *Visitations* premiered at Bing Concert Hall at Stanford University in 2013, directed by Rinde Eckert, and received its New York City premiere at the Prototype Festival in 2014. Originally from New York, O'Brien lives in Los Angeles with his wife and daughter. Website: danobrien.org.

Quetzal Flores is a Grammy® Award winning East LA Chican@ rock group. Now celebrating its 20-year anniversary, Quetzal is the collaborative project of Quetzal Flores (guitar), Martha González (lead vocals, percussion), Tylana Enomoto (violin), Juan Pérez (bass), Peter Jacobson (cello), and Alberto Lopez (percussion). The musical ensemble is influenced by an East LA rock soundscape composed of Mexican ranchera, cumbia, salsa, rock, R&B, folk, and fusions of international musics, and also one whose political vision is based in social activism, feminism, and the belief that there is radical potential in expressive culture. During the past two decades, the musical force of Quetzal has created a unique cultural platform that has sounded against conditions of oppression and marginalization. On the twentieth anniversary of their first flight, Quetzal introduces us to another sphere of being, one that challenges us to reimagine human life in relation to the other forms of life that we are so often connected to and through.

ZIMMERMAN. Hello?
Hello?
We've had a few break-ins
in the neighborhood,
and here comes this guy

looking like he's up to no good.

Looking like he's on drugs or whatever.
It's pouring rain
and he's just walking round.

What race is he? – Black.
What's he wearing?
A hoodie
and blue jeans, white tennis shoes.

He's staring at me,
at all the houses.

Why's he staring at me?

Where am I?
Retreat,
Retreat,
Retreat,
Retreat at Twin Lakes...

Retreat,
Retreat at Twin Lakes...

He's coming towards me
with his hand in his waistband.

[ZIMMERMAN plays the guitar. No need for a cell phone or, for the time being, the gun.]

He's a black guy
for sure.

There's definitely something wrong
with him.

He's coming back to check me out again
with something in his hands.

How long till you get here?
Because these assholes
always get away.

– Shit,

now he's running.
Which way's he running?
I'm running after him.
I don't need to do that.
What's my name?
George.
Last name
Zimmerman.

I don't know where this kid's
gone.

Hello?
Hello?

TRAYVON.   Why you running after me?

ZIMMERMAN. Why are you here?

TRAYVON.   I can't be?

ZIMMERMAN. Why aren't you running
in out of the rain?

TRAYVON.   I got this hoodie to keep me dry.

ZIMMERMAN. Let me see your face.

TRAYVON.   Why?

ZIMMERMAN. You can see mine.

TRAYVON.   Barely, barely.

ZIMMERMAN. What's that
in your hand?

TRAYVON.   Show me yours and I'll show you
mine.

ZIMMERMAN. Punks have been stealing.

TRAYVON.   What punks?

ZIMMERMAN. Black punks
that look like you.
It's a fact.

TRAYVON.   It's a fact
you look like a skinhead, or a pervert
of some kind. – That earring,
man!

ZIMMERMAN. I'm married,
man.

TRAYVON.   Not for long.

ZIMMERMAN. If it were light
you'd see my face.

                I'm Hispanic.

My mother is
Peruvian. Her mother was half-black
like you.

TRAYVON.   I'm all black, ese.

ZIMMERMAN. Mi abuela
watching Sabado Gigante, cooking
Papa a la Huancaína.

TRAYVON.   Fuck is that?

ZIMMERMAN. Potatoes in cream sauce… Mmm…

I've protested
police brutality against the homeless
black guys.

I took a black girl to the prom.

I voted for Obama!

Obama, Obama, 'bama, Obama,
Obama, 'bama, Obama, Obama,
'bama, Obama, Obama, 'bama…

TRAYVON.   Why you acting white then, Zimmerman?

ZIMMERMAN. How do you know my name?

TRAYVON.   Is Zimmerman a Jewish name?
Zimmerman, Zimmerman, Zimmerman…

ZIMMERMAN. I was an altar boy
in my youth. But I wasn't molested
by priests. Once even got arrested
when I was your age, for punching
this white cop who was trying to shake down
my drunk friend.

TRAYVON.   Did you do time?

ZIMMERMAN. My father
was the reason.

TRAYVON.   The reason?

ZIMMERMAN. The reason I got off: Judge
Zimmerman.

TRAYVON.   Zimmerman, Zimmerman,
Zimmerman, Judge Zimmerman…

Zimmerman, Zimmerman,
that's not why you're here now.

ZIMMERMAN. I had a girl
I just could not let go.
Came to her house
when she called.
When she pushed me I pushed her
back harder.

TRAYVON.   Zimmerman, Zimmerman,
Zimmerman, Zimmerman…

ZIMMERMAN. I used to fool around with
my cousin. She was six,
I was eight. We were in love, lying
on the floor
with the whole family…

TRAYVON.   Zimmerman, Zimmerman,
Zimmerman, Zimmerman…

ZIMMERMAN. Watching TV, blankets all around…

TRAYVON.   Zimmerman, Zimmerman,
                 Zimmerman, Zimmerman...

ZIMMERMAN. She never said a thing.
                No one would've believed her
                if she did.

                Certain people
                don't believe certain people.

TRAYVON.   – I'm scared of you.

ZIMMERMAN. That's funny. I'm afraid
                of people like you.

TRAYVON.   If you're so afraid
                then why am I the one who has to run
                away?

ZIMMERMAN. Because I've got the gun,
                because I've got the gun.
                One of us is going to die tonight
                because I've got the gun.

TRAYVON.   Because you've got the gun,
                because you've got the gun.
                One of us is going to die tonight
                because you've got the gun.

ZIMMERMAN. If you carried a gun
                legally like me, you'd be safe
                right now.

                If you carried guns
                like this one. Kel-Tec
                .9 mm subcompact. Easy
                to hide in your underwear. Not much fun
                to shoot. Only a few feet away and
                I'd miss you.

But when you're on top of me
pounding my head against the stone, I bet my gun's
going to set me free.

TRAYVON. Because you've got the gun,
because you've got the gun.
One of us is going to die tonight
because you've got the gun.

But why
you hate me, son? We should be together
on this. We're both middle-class and shit. Middle-class
and living in this shit-hole.

ZIMMERMAN. You live here?

TRAYVON. I'm visiting.

ZIMMERMAN. No, I'm nothing like you!
A hood. Drooping pants.
Been expelled five times
in one year.
Jewelry in the bag
at school.

Where's your mother? Where's your father?

Where's your God damned respect?
Why you smoking
dope and bragging about it?

Why the golden
teeth?   *[TRAYVON
                                          is shot.]*

Why can't you try just a bit harder
to be me?

TRAYVON.   Zimmerman. A wannabe
              white man!

ZIMMERMAN.   Zimmerman, Zimmerman,
              Zimmerman, Zimmerman...

TRAYVON.   Zimmerman, Zimmerman,
              Zimmerman, Zimmerman...

ZIMMERMAN.   Because I've got the gun...   *[The* **OFFICER**
                                              arrives on the scene.
TRAYVON.   Now is when I run at him...   *She carries*
                                              ZIMMERMAN's
ZIMMERMAN.   Because I've got the gun...   *gun.]*

TRAYVON.   And pop his nose like a balloon...

ZIMMERMAN.   One of us is going to die tonight...

TRAYVON.   A punching and a kicking...

ZIMMERMAN.   Because I've got the gun...

TRAYVON.   Hand grabs
              the barrel like a lover...
ZIMMERMAN.   Because I've got the gun...

TRAYVON.   Help! Help!

ZIMMERMAN.   Because I've got the gun...

TRAYVON.   Help! Help! Shit...

ZIMMERMAN.   One of us is going to die tonight...

TRAYVON.   Help! Help! Help! Help!

ZIMMERMAN.   Because I've got the gun...

TRAYVON.   Help! Help! Help!

ZIMMERMAN. Because I've got the gun…

TRAYVON.   Help! Help!

ZIMMERMAN. Because I've got the gun…

TRAYVON.   Help! Help!

ZIMMERMAN. One of us is going to die tonight…

TRAYVON.   Help…!

ZIMMERMAN. Because I've got the gun…

OFFICER.   Zimmerman.
                 Zimmerman,
                 you're free.

                 You're free to go.

                 Your house arrest
                 is over.

                 A jury of women ruled
                 you did your best.

                 It's a crazy old mixed-up world.

                 Hello?
                 Hello?

                 Zimmerman,
                 you seem distracted.

Give us the bracelet
from round your ankle, and we'll give you back
this gun.

The Equalizer.

This Kel-Tec
.9 mm subcompact. Easy
to hide in your underwear. Not much fun
to shoot. Only a few feet away and
I'd miss you.

But when you're on top of me
pounding my head against the stone, I bet
this gun would set me free.

But Zimmerman,
poor innocent Zimmerman...

These assholes
always get away.

Not this time. Not this time, right

Zimmerman?

End of Play

Dressing

Mona Mansour
& Tala Manassah

CAST

MOM – early 40s, black
SON – 17, black

SETTING

Their kitchen, his room, and other places, more suggested than literal.

The scenes should feel both realistic and abstract. The clothes should be real.

ABOUT THE PLAYWRIGHTS

Mona Mansour's play *The Way West* had its world premiere in spring of 2014 at Steppenwolf, directed by Amy Morton. The play received the 2013 Sky Cooper New American Play Prize from Marin Theatre Company, where it will get its West Coast premiere in April 2015. The play received a BareBones workshop at the Lark Play Development Center (directed by Linsay Firman), where Mona was a Fellow in 2012. *The Hour of Feeling* (directed by Mark Wing-Davey) received its world premiere in the 2012 Humana Festival in Louisville. Following that, it was part of the High Tide Festival in the U.K. as part of the Rifle Hall plays. *Urge for Going* (directed by Hal Brooks) received a LAB production in the 2011 season at the Public Theater, and had its West Coast premiere at San Francisco's Golden Thread (directed by Evren Odcikin). *The Vagrant,* the third play in the trilogy, was commissioned by the Public Theater and workshopped at the 2013 Sundance Theater Institute with Mark Wing-Davey directing. Mona was a member of the Public Theater's Emerging Writers Group, a Core Writer at Minneapolis' Playwrights' Center, and is now a member of New Dramatists. Other plays include *Across the Water, Girl Scouts of America* and *Broadcast Yourself* (part of Headlong Theater's Decade). With Tala Manassah she has written *The House,* for Noor Theatre, *After,* and *The Letter,* which premiered in November 2012 at Golden Thread's ReOrient Festival; Mona and Tala were in residence at Berkeley Rep's Ground Floor, where they worked on a musical play called *The Wife.* They were given an Ensemble Studio Theatre/Sloan commission to write a play about 1970s Iraq. Other commissions include *Unseen,* a play for South Coast Rep's inaugural Crossroads program. 2012 Whiting Award. 2014 Middle East America Playwright Award. monamansour.com

Tala Jamal Manassah is deputy executive director of Morningside Center for Teaching Social Responsibility, the national leader in school-based social and emotional learning programs. Morningside Center works for a society that is just, peaceful, and truly democratic by working in schools, hand in hand with educators, to make schools joyful, productive spaces where young people develop a rigorous sense of social responsibility. Under her leadership, Morningside Center has undertaken the largest school-based expansion of restorative practices in the U.S. As of March 2014, the program has impacted educators from 150 middle schools and high schools throughout New York City. She was recently invited by NYC Mayor Bill de Blasio's office to join the administration's Leadership Team on School Climate and Discipline. As a playwright, she has co-written, with Mona Mansour, *The House,* commissioned by NYC's Noor Theater and the American Institute for Architecture and read as part of their Building ANew series in March 2012; The Letter, a short play that premiered in November 2012 in San Francisco as part of Golden Thread's ReOrient Festival; and After, a full-length play that was produced at Queens College in 2013. Manassah and Mansour were awarded a residency at Berkeley Rep's Ground Floor in 2013 to develop a musical play called *The Wife.* Manassah holds an A.B. and A.M. from the University of Chicago.

(At top, they are in a kitchen. It's morning.)

*(**SON** says this very small bit to audience, or maybe to **MOM**, or both.)*

SON. Part one:

He's off to school.

His pants hang low – not like off his ass. No one's doing that anymore.

This is an issue.

*(**MOM** has grabbed a belt loop on his pants, which hang low but not like off his ass! And now they speak to each other, only. They have fun. They like this.)*

MOM. This is an issue.

SON. No.

MOM. Do you know where it came from?

SON. What came from?

MOM. This style, this –

SON. I know. Ma, this again?

MOM. Symbol. It's a symbol of –

SON. I know. Prison. Prisoners aren't allowed to have belts. See? I remember.

MOM. Right. And the pants sag. Which even just symbolically plays into –

SON. School-to-prison pipeline, all that.

MOM. Exactly.

(Beat.)

SON. But I have a 3.8.

(Another beat. They both smile. He pulls his pants up showily, the smallest bit to appease her.)

Okay?

MOM. I just worry.

SON. About what?

MOM. A million things! People not taking you seriously. That's one thing.

SON. Are you not paying attention? In this birthday suit, sometimes it doesn't matter what you're wearing.

MOM. Stop it, that's so defeatist. That's not even an original thought!

SON. In this case, if it was original, it wouldn't be so true.

(Over a white tank, he puts on a T-shirt. It's one of those Threadless Ts, the kind of thing that has some hip and very insidery design on it.)

MOM. And what is this?

SON. A T-shirt.

MOM. Of what?

SON. I don't know. A robot.

MOM. Doing what?

SON. Mom, it's not that deep.

MOM. What is the robot doing?

(Not totally sure himself, He pulls the shirt away from his body to check:)

SON. Beating up a COKE CAN.

MOM. *(under)* Hm.

SON. It's just a cool shirt! – This is a boring life you lead, Mom.

MOM. There's nothing really clever about it. Is it a symbol for something?

SON. Um, I would say… It's a symbol for a robot beating up a can of Coke.

MOM. But why? What did the can of Coke do to deserve that?

SON. *(laughing)* Come on Mom. Just leave it, please.

MOM. It feels symbolic to me. A competition over who has the best armor.

SON. I'm gonna jet. Eat later, okay?

MOM. I still don't understand why you can't wear the ones I got you.

SON. The button-up-the-front things?

MOM. Those.

SON. Yeah. Not today, unfortunately.

MOM. Why is that?

SON. Another day.

(He's bullshitting. She knows it, he knows she knows it, they play the game anyway:)

MOM. Um-hmm, when's that?

SON. When I turn into a Jehovah's Witness and go door to door selling Bibles.

(He laughs.)

MOM. Oh he thinks that's so funny.

SON. I mean yeah, kinda.

MOM. You know it's rude, right? Not to even let me see you in them? Those were gifts!

SON. Gifts? Gifts? That's what you're supposed to do as a mom. Buy me shit.

MOM. Oh is THAT so?

SON. Yep. Love you, Ma.

(And with that, the SON leaves.)

(MOM is left alone. And now she speaks to the audience, or depending on how this is staged, she speaks to the audience and the actor who played the SON, who maybe sits at the side now.)

MOM. Part two.

No. Not part two.

Not doing that. Not yet. I can't.

(And then:)

I'm gonna – Just talk for a minute. About other things. Easier for all of us, right?

(Beat.)

I used to take him to tae kwon do – I'd stand with all the other parents in the window, watching, these wiggly little bodies punching, you know, they look ridiculous. And it's the same routine every time. But you stand there. These parents who say EVERY THING THEIR CHILD DOES IS MAGICAL? They are lying. And I mean, I coulda done other things with my time. We both could have. But you want to create a foundation.

Give him that mental-physical discipline.

So once when he was like eight or so, I left to take a call, I'm gone fifteen minutes, maybe?, I come back, and suddenly he's doing these kicks, these crazy double kicks. He's two feet off the ground Suddenly: Everything's coordinated. He's like a little pro. Now how did that happen? Two years of these lessons and nothing seems to click.

And I think:

Was I watching him too hard?

Did my leaving help him to make that leap? Did he need me to stop watching just so he could stretch that way?

You have to be able to look away, to turn around, to let go. But how?

(And she says, she doesn't want to, but she says –)

Part Two.

The mother gets a phone call.

(We hear three loud pops.)

(A beat, or a couple beats…)

You have to go see – Someone drives you.

And as they drive you remember the pain of childbirth, the tenuousness of those first moments, you remember small eyes, and small gasps, and the very tiny hands that reached for you. Tiny hands, reaching.

You don't remember how you got here.

To this building. But somehow you know exactly where to go.

Cause we've been doing this dance, right? We know how to this! We know where to go, we know how to behave! And they take you into this room, and then another one, and another one, and your legs move, something primordial moves you forward, and you dig your nails into your hands so you won't feel anything, and it's not YOUR body that moves you forward. It's – that body, the one that's in your core.

THIS is thing that you have been carrying. Always carrying.

It's all going forward now, you don't want it to be, it's going forward, time, and your body, you have no choice. And finally: There it is… And there it is… And there it is.

(Long Beat. She's back at home. In his room? Or at least with his clothes. She's folding them, maybe, maybe folding them and putting them in a pile?)

Part Three.

She goes to his room, she folds his clothes.

I used to go into his closet and move these three shirts – button up the front ones – I'd put put them in the front, like he would suddenly see them and realize he wanted to wear them. Like moving the okra on his plate so he'd want to eat it – "See how good this looks?" Ridiculous.

It's not about class. It was never about that. Me trying to get him dressed up so we could elevate him in other people's eyes. Not really.

The clothes, It's – you do these things, these small things to protect his –

protect his –

his –

(She breaks –)

Body. That body.
Oh.

(handles with the clothes in some way)

Oh, vulnerable body.
I thought I knew. How much.
Oh.
I heard someone on – you know, some panel, say this thing: Men in black bodies have since the founding of this country been vulnerable by way of the body that they inhabit. Oh. That's a crazy thing to think about, that's a crazy thing to carry. For him.

Right?

(And now she holds one of the shirts.)

And this – these – never were going to protect him. Were they? Why did I think they could?

(Clarity. Beyond pain. Exhaustion. Beat.)

And now I will do another dance.

With other mothers, some that I know on a molecular level, and some who live in places I don't even know exist. I would like to know those women, but not in this way. This is an involuntary and wicked dance.

(She's alone with the shirt, maybe a song comes on.)

End of Play

No More Monsters Here

Marcus Gardley

"There are no monsters here"
– Don West, George Zimmerman's Attorney

CHARACTERS

REBECCA – a white woman

DOC – a black psychiatrist. The same actor plays **EMPLOYER**

GREATEST GRAND – The same actor plays **OOKIE**, a dealer

ABOUT THE PLAYWRIGHT

Marcus Gardley is a poet-playwright who is the current recipient of the 2014 Glickman Award. He was the 2013 USA James Baldwin Fellow and the 2011 PEN Laura Pels award winner for Mid-Career Playwright. *The New Yorker* describes Gardley as "the heir to Garcia Lorca, Pirandello and Tennessee Williams." His play *The House that Will Not Stand* was commissioned and produced by Berkeley Rep and had subsequent productions at Yale Rep and the Tricycle Theater in London. He is an ensemble member playwright at Victory Gardens Theater where his play *The Gospel of Loving Kindness* was produced in March and won the 2015 BTAA award for best play/playwright. In 2014, his saga *The Road Weeps, the Well Runs Dry* about the migration of Black Seminoles (a tribe of African American and First Nations People) from Florida to Oklahoma had a national tour. He has had several productions, some of which include: *Every Tongue Confess* at Arena Stage starring Phylicia Rashad and directed by Kenny Leon and *On The Levee*, which premiered in 2010 at LCT3. He is the recipient of the 2011 Aetna New Voice Fellowship at Hartford Stage, the Hellen Merrill Award, a Kellsering Honor and the Gerbode Emerging Playwright Award. He holds an MFA in Playwriting from the Yale Drama School and is a member of The Dramatists Guild. Gardley is a professor of Theater and Performance Studies at Brown University.

(A black psychiatrist looks over a patient's file. The patient is a white woman. She lies on a chaise.)

REBECCA. What's up, Doc? You look worried. What's the diagnosis? Am I insane? I'm insane, aren't I?

DOC. Insane is such a strong word, Rebecca. I wouldn't say you're <u>in</u> "sane." I'd say you're half out of your gourd. You're what we psychiatrists like to call a touch cray cray.

REBECCA. Oh God, does that mean I'm bipolar? I knew it! I'm bi and I like to work the pole. I knew I was bi-polar. I'm two times the crazy. I'm my mother.

DOC. No, no, no. Calm down. You're not bi-polar.

REBECCA. Then I'm schizophrenic!? I got four voices in my head instead of two? No decent man's going to marry me now. I got four personalities. Who wants to marry four people – I'll have to start dating a bigamist. A Mormon. Is Mitt Romney still married to that bitch that makes ketchup?

DOC. Rebecca, will you take a deep breath. What you have is totally normal…unfortunately. It's nothing to be stupid about, plus there is a cure.

REBECCA. Oh. Cool! I get to pop pills. Holla! What I got doc?

DOC. You have negroidphobia.

REBECCA. Hold the phone. I got negro what?

DOC. Negroidphobia. It's a fear of people of African descent primarily black men. Just as arachnophobia is a fear of spiders and alektorophobia is a fear of chickens and cyclophobia is a fear of bikes and genuphobia is a fear of kneecaps, you have Negroidphobia which is a fear of nig –

REBECCA. – Shut the black gate, are you saying I hate black people! That's a black face lie! One of my neighbors is Africans Americans. We've walked our Chihuahuas together during a sunset. I've had her over the house for quiche. Plus, I have two Nina Simone CDs and I know the theme song to the Fresh Prince of Bell Air. How can I be racist?

DOC. Nobody's sayin you're a racist, Becky. I mean, you are but nobody's sayin it to your face although it kinda goes without saying. Racism implies that you see a culture as inferior or superior to another. It is a bi-product of privilege. No one can cure that shit but Jesus. What you have is more specific.

REBECCA. I'm offended.

DOC. Wow. You fear black men because you have bought into the myth that they are violent and you're the one that is offended. Classic projection.

(He writes on his pad.)

REBECCA. This is going to sound racist, cliché and ignorant but honestly one of my best friends is a black.

DOC. Ooo, and delusional. Nice, Ann Coulter. Keep talking out the side of your neck.

(He writes more feverishly.)

REBECCA. My girl Shoronda at my job – I work at the post office – we besties. We got a secret handshake, she taught me how to twerk before Miley got on the VMA's, I ate chicken at her church one Easter, plus she lets me touch her hair.

DOC. I guess Doctor King's Dream has been fully realized then, hunh? WAKE UP! Nobody is saying that you hate blacks, Beckka. Stay with me on this one, I have a degree! I'm saying you fear blacks. You failed our fear of a black planet test, twice. When a black man walks passed your car, you admitted to locking the door and turning on your car alarm.

REBECCA. Yeah but I wasn't locking it because he was black. I was locking it because he looked scary.

DOC. Exactly! And when you get in an elevator with a black man, you admitted to clutching your purse nervously and holding your breath until you've had a chance to get off.

REBECCA. Yes but that's because I don't want them to trip over my bag. I've heard that black men have big feet. And I carry a big bag. And everybody knows what big feet mean…near big bags. They'll trip. They will trip over my big bag with their big feet and then rape me. Feel me? *(beat.)* Oh god, I'm trippin, aren't I? I… I really do fear black men. Sweet Jesus, I've become my father.

(She cries.)

DOC. There, there, there, Beckett. It's okay. The first step to recovery is admitting you're fucked up. You came to me because you've been having nightmares about Favor Flav hiding in your closet and playing with your alarm clock. This fear you have is real and really fucked up. But a lot of Caucazoids have it. And that's why I invented a cure. It's in its experimental stages but so far it has helped a significant number of whites who have undergone treatment. The process only takes a few days and if you're unsatisfied we will give you your money back or admit you to a mental hospital.

REBECCA. This shit sounds expensive. Thank God, I have Obamacare. What do I have to do?

DOC. It's simple. You just have to put on this hoodie and live in the hood for three days as a black man.

(DOC hands her a black hoodie.)

REBECCA. Um…what you talkin about Willis? You ain't for real, are you…

DOC. Yup, I'm for sheezy. Check out this hoodie. It looks like any ole black hoodie but it's actually a state of the art transformational mask. Using holographic imaging, it forms a unique black face to cover your own. If you wear it, it will make you look like a black man to all who gaze upon you. No one will assume that you are a white woman behind the mask. You will be black and literally walk in another man's shoes for three days. This will no doubt cure you of your negroidphobia. Trust me, it's surefire. Go ahead put it on. We can begin your treatment immediately.

REBECCA. Oh, I don't know. Shouldn't I have time to think about this first? What if something happens to me in the hood? What if I get hoodwinked, bamboozled and held at gunpoint?

DOC. Nonsense, we're going to place you in Harlem. There's more white folks there than in Europe. Be brave, Rebbie. Don't you want to be a fully evolved, open-minded human being for your race?

REBECCA. Well, I want to be well doctor.

DOC. Good. Then let's get you hood.

(She quickly puts on the hood.)

You'll also need to sag your jeans and wear these Tims.

(He hands her more items.)

A cultural ambassador will help you change your walk and voice and attempt to teach you how to do the Harlem Shake. In time, no one will notice old Rebecca from the new Raheem. Good luck and God speed.

(They shake. Then he Harlem shakes as he exits. She gets dressed and practices her walk. It is ridiculous. Lights cross fade to show a passing of time. Twenty-four hours later, **GREATEST GRAND** *enters. She is 162, hunched over to her toes, her wig has food in it and she has a walker, which has headlights and a horn. She wears a nightgown and dirty bunny slippers that are missing one ear and an eye. She wakes* **REBECCA** *who has become* **RAHEEM***.)*

GREATEST GRAND. Rise and shine, Raheem. Breakfast is the most imported meal of the day. Gots to eat. Gots to eat black food if you wants to uplift the race.

RAHEEM. Uh… I ain't hungry, granny. I'll get somethin later.

GREATEST GRAND. Ain't hungry!? Why? Have you gotten too good for soul food? I send you to that good school to gets an edumacation and you got too good for chitlins. Oprah eats chitlins! You see her thighs! That's a bitch that will fuck up a chitlin! You gettin brand new, Raheem.

RAHEEM. No, I'm not new. I'm the same ole Raheem, Granny. I promise.

GREATEST GRAND. Then you must not be feeling well. Steel grievin over Ray Ray's death? Shugar, don't you know you live in the hood? You might as well face the fact that a lot of your homies are gonna get got at a young age. Hell, you 18. You lucky you still livin your damn self. The black man is an endangered species, baby and yo ass is in danger.

RAHEEM. That's a bit of an exaggeration isn't it? I mean, I see a lot of brothers hanging on the street corner. On the basketball court, at the club. They chillin in the cut on the regular.

GREATEST GRAND. No, they're getting cut down on the regular. If you ever did a body count, if you ever waded through the blood, you'd know how much danger you're really in. If the cops don't shoot you or some random dude on neighborhood watch doesn't stand his ground on your corpse, or another brother with beef doesn't shoot you to assert his manhood then a stray bullet with no doubt take you out. Many bodies get laid to rest on the daily because the black male body is the great American sacrifice. History has had it hanging from trees, chained to gangs, burnt to bones and the future's got it slavin behind bars. It must be put out of sight. Cause you're public enemy number one. Black president or not, you still a nigga in the night, when you go knockin on a stranger's door after your car has crashed and the cops have been called – you still put the fear of God into even the good, hippy, free love, liberal minded folk. Cause they all have drunk the kool-aid and swore it was just Starbucks. The media, the TV, the movies, hell even hip hop makes you out to be a bad ass muther fucker. But it ain't real. It's just story. Stereotypes typed up into stereo for a nation sick with slave guilt. It feeds their inner demons but you can take yourself out of the myth. You can take your life and rewrite it, Raheem. You must create a future for yourself that is bigger – better than this story you were told to buy into. Ergo baby, you need to get a fuckin job.

(She throws a dress coat over him and hands him a tie. He puts it on.)

I spent the last of my social security to get you this suit. Don't disappoint me now, hear. *(sweet)* Or granny's gonna beat that ass, baby.

*(Lights crossfade to **DOC** who is now dressed in a Walmart uniform. He is **EMPLOYER**.)*

EMPLOYER. According to your resume, you have no marketable skills. You've never even held a job before.

RAHEEM. I know but I can't hold down a job if someone doesn't hand one to me.

EMPLOYER. Well, my hands are tied. I can't afford to take a chance on anybody right now –

RAHEEM. – Who says that I'm a chance? I could be the best employee you ever had.

EMPLOYER. Fat chance: your resume has misspellings, you arrived thirty-three minutes late to your interview and you have no references.

RAHEEM. Yeah but this is Walmart. You got old, dying people greeting folks at the door. You sell low quality products made by children in third world countries for poor people in the U.S. many of whom are on welfare. Why you actin like this the Banana Republic? I just want a job, man. I'm tryin to bag groceries. Let's keep it real. I can say paper or plastic with a smile. Check this: *(He smiles.)* Paper? Plastic?

EMPLOYER. Yeah see, this is not going to work. I don't think you posses the Walmart spirit.

RAHEEM. Look, my grandmother spent the last of her social security check to get me this suit. She got her hopes up and she hardly ever has any hopes so when she does get them up, I like for her to keep them up. Just so she has something to reach for.

EMPLOYER. That's precious. We'll call you if something becomes available. In the meantime, I suggest you find a career more suitable to your work experience.

(Lights crossfade to GREATEST GRAND who is now a street thug named OOKIE. She has on baggy jeans, a plaid shirt, doo rag and some garden gloves he sits on a hydrant.)

OOKIE. Yo, son I heard you lookin for work. Pray tell, what's your five-year plan, homie?

RAHEEM. Five-year plan? I'm just tryin to make it to tomorrow. Tryin to pay my Granny back for a suit she bought me.

OOKIE. That's touchin B but you need a five-year plan, dawg. Don't you read Suze Orman?

RAHEEM. Uh, nawl. Who dat?

OOKIE. Bitch just the shit, nephew. She got mad strategies for a secure financial future. Last year she had me investing in a mutual fund with a fifty-nine percent return, plus she diversified my stock portfolio and improved by individual retirement account over three years with a fixed annuity. I'm going to retire in like six years, move to the Congo and live among the pigmies. Bet.

RAHEEM. Wait, you got a retirement account and you sell drugs?

OOKIE. Pharmaceuticals, nigga. Drugs got a negative connotation. I sell pharmaceuticals. Man, you need to read Iyanla Vanzant. I feel like you judging me hella hard right now.

RAHEEM. Well, I was thinking of going to college.

OOKIE. College!? You stupid Corn Nut's brother Nachos, got a degree from CUNY and right now he workin at the Starbucks on 125th. I make ten times what he make and I don't pay Uncle Sam a penny. Open your eyes cuz, colleges have become corporations. You want to make real money, you got to have an entrepreneurial spirit. You got to focus on product. You got to sell trees.

(**OOKIE** *hands him several very large sandwich bags stuffed with marijuana.*)

RAHEEM. Oh, I don't know. I'm not really good with plants. I hear the NYPD is giving brothers ten years just for dime bags. Plus, I don't think I could handle prison, I'm too pretty. I'm like a masculine Halle Berry.

(**RAHEEM** *shows her profile. Time.*)

OOKIE. You'll make over 500 hundred dollars a day.

RAHEEM. OMG! Count me in. When can I start?

(**RAHEEM** *takes the weed and stuffs it in his pockets.*)

OOKIE. Today. I'm giving you some merchandise cause your story touched me and… I hardly ever get touched… *(sexual)* I haven't been touched in so long. Plus, I know you just trying to help your granny out so…do me a favor and don't get caught. Try not to be so…how do I put this…black.

RAHEEM. Right. I'll see what I can do.

(*Night falls instantly. The stage is dimly lit.* **RAHEEM** *walks the streets. He tries not to walk so black, he tries to remember how he walked when he was* **REBECCA** *but he can't. She can't. He walks. He is being followed by someone. He walks faster – the figure follows him. Eventually, he stops. The figure stops.*)

RAHEEM. Who's following me? Stop being an asshole and show yourself. I ain't no punk, I'll bust a cap in dat ass. Show yourself, I said! *(Silence.)* I shoulda known better than makin a drop off in the suburbs. Bitches here be playa hatin. Aight Raheem, relax. Play it cool, homes. Be Rebecca. Try not to stand out. This is your last day in this hoodie. Last day wearin this mask. Just try to get through the night.

*(Again, he walks. He tries to walk white. He can't do it. The figure follows again. He runs. The figure runs. They run in circles. The movement is stylized. Eventually, **RAHEEM** falls and the figure falls on top of him. The figure is covered head to toe in black. We cannot make out a face. **RAHEEM** fights the figure. He slams his head against the sidewalk. The fight is hard to watch. Eventually the figure breaks free and pulls a gun from his pants. The figure stands over **RAHEEM** and points the gun at him. **REBECCA** screams. We see a lightning speed projection of the following faces/images: Medgar Evers, Emmit Till, Oscar Grant, Sean Bell, Amidou Diallo and lynched black men.)*

Wait! Hold on! I'm not Raheem, I'm not black. I'm Rebecca. I'm a white.

*(**REBECCA** tries to take the hoodie off but cannot. For some reason, it's stuck.)*

I'm Rebecca Smith. This is just an experiment, a cure. Please! Please sir don't…don't shoot. Things are not as they seem. I'm not as I… I'm a…

*(The figure cocks his gun, **REBECCA** releases a piercing scream! He shoots. **REBECCA** grabs her heart, she wails. She flails on the ground holding her heart. She weeps bloody murder as lights slowly rise on her. When lights come up full, the figure takes his mask off. It is **DOC**. He kneels, embraces **REBECCA**. She cries in his arms.)*

DOC. It's okay. It's okay Rebecca Smith. It was just a simulation. You are not shot. You are not bleeding. It was not real. You are well now. You are healed.

(She breaks from his embrace. She tears off the hoodie and throws it at him.)

REBECCA. Fuck you! FUCK YOU, DOC!!!!

DOC. You're welcome?

REBECCA. That was not fair! That was not okay! I felt it. I felt the bullet go though me, okay. I felt them. In me.

(She cries.)

DOC. Them?

REBECCA. Those men. Why'd you do that? Why you make me feel them; their pain. I saw their faces. It was inhumane. It was fucked... SO FUCKED!!!!!

DOC. I have no idea what you're talking about. There are no men, Rebeck –

REBECCA. DON'T LIE TO ME! You used me! Got into my fuckin head. They're in my fuckin head, still. Whispering. Their mad! I'M SO MAD!

DOC. It's just a side affect, Mrs. Smith. Trust me, you are healed. You are better.

REBECCA. I don't want to be better. I want them out of my head.

DOC. Look, please calm down. I still want to run a few test.

REBECCA. NO! Hell no! I will no longer be your test rat. This treatment should be banned. You should have your licensed revoked. This is racist!

*(**REBECCA** grabs her coat and purse.)*

DOC. Wow. Okay. So I guess you won't be recommending me to your friends.

*(**REBECCA** screams in frustration then exits slamming the door. **DOC** scratches his head. **REBECCA** walks into an elevator. We hear delightful elevator music. She pushes a button and watches impatiently for the elevator to go to the first floor. It stops at the third. A white woman gets on. She looks at **REBECCA** and gives her a half smile then moves to the farthest side away from her. **REBECCA** ponders this, then looks at the woman.*

*The woman becomes frightened and turns her face away,
slowly clutching her purse to her breast, holding her
breath, biting her lip. Time.* **REBECCA** *folds her arms.
She feels small. Time. She looks at her face in the elevator
mirror – she touches her lips, her cheek and nose. Could
she still be black? She wipes away a real tear. Elevator
music still plays. Lights fade to black. Damn.)*